Griselda,

50p

Close Encounters of the Traveling Kind

Stories of near death adventures around the world

Amanda Jayne

Happy Travels,

GW00706160

WALDORF PUBLISHING

Much love

Amanda
Jayne
x

Published by Waldorf Publishing
2140 Hall Johnson Road
#102-345
Grapevine, Texas 76051
www.WaldorfPublishing.com

Close Encounters of the Traveling Kind
Stories of near death adventures around the world

ISBN: 978-1-64255-679-7
Library of Congress Control Number: 2018933794
Copyright © 2018

Table of Contents

Dedication

To all my traveling companions

especially Svenya and the people of Langtang

who have traveled further

than the rest of us so far.

And to Mrs Joseph for your stories

and your inspiration

Introduction

Mrs Joseph wasn't like the other teachers in my school, they were busy giving me detentions, worrying about the length of my skirt, whether I was wearing the regulation green knickers and whether it really was me who'd (inadvertently) flooded the bathroom. Mrs Joseph didn't care about those things, she was busy telling me exotic travel stories and teaching me that no matter what seemingly hopeless situations I found myself in, if I could stay calm, curious and free from worry, then something would always turn up to help me. She was about four foot nine, had a face wider than it was long and thick, dark, straw hair, a bouffant drawn back in such a way that it looked like a wig. Originally from Burma, she had lived much of her childhood in India having being forced to leave her home country as a refugee. She also had a penchant for getting run over and at various points throughout the school year she would tell us stories of her latest altercation with a car. As a result of these, one leg was shorter than the other, the sole of her shoe built up with an ever-increasing orthopaedic layer. She never seemed to mind her near misses, or the ones that hit, and had an attitude to life that fascinated me. I loved listening to stories of her travels as well as her car accidents and the freak flukes that always happened to save her. I loved her exotic accent and mimicked it in fun and admiration. I loved her easy attitude to life, her enticing travel stories and her insistence that whatever you needed would turn up at exactly the right time. If it wasn't there I didn't need it, she assured me.

It was because of her that I promised myself I would go to all those places I longed to see. I would spend hours pouring over a large book of 'Mysterious Places' of the world. These were pre-google days, so the only information (besides Mrs Joseph) I had access to lay across these pages. Their huge colorful photos called out to me to come and see them in all their glory and because of my beloved English teacher, I went.

These are a few of the stories from those travels, adventures that reinforced what Mrs Joseph had taught me. Things really do turn up right when you need them, I have tested the theory many times and have no choice but to agree with her. I often revisit these events because they are a source of learning that continues to help me move through life, but more than that, they make me laugh. Except the South Africa story, that wasn't funny.

I hope you enjoy reading them as much as I enjoyed writing them.

ELEMENTAL MISTAKES
Mᴛ Fᴜᴊɪ, Japan, 2002

Reasons for near-death:
Ignoring all advice on mountains and mountain
sickness; Stupidity.

I had agreed to climb Mt Fuji during a night of drunken revelry.

It began at the Karaoke Box, where a vat of cheap whisky helped us work our way through a wealth of soft rock, bad noodles and easy listening greats. Someone came up with the idea that coming to live in Japan and *not* climbing Mt Fuji was rude. Everyone agreed heartily, and it was decided that the gaijin (which is what Japanese call foreigners) English teachers would climb as a group. I say 'it was decided' because I'm not sure where I was when the agreement was made, most probably somewhere inside an enthusiastic rendition of *I will survive.* Or in the bathroom. Suffice to say, when it came to making the actual arrangements the following day, the enthusiastic climbing party swiftly whittled down from a throng of English teachers to a party of two.

John and I briefly looked up some information about the climb and I immediately got lost in stories of Lady Parkes, who (in 1868 at a time when women were prohibited from climbing Mt Fuji by law) nipped up the volcano, pursued by a foray of angry men. My eyes grew wide as I read, imagining I was Parkes trying desperately to make it to the top before they caught me. It was a fascinating story and I found her courage inspiring. So much so, I didn't really check out much else and once we'd discovered that it was best to start in the evening and climb through the night, we felt ready.

The idea of climbing in the evening is that you arrive at the summit in the early hours. This way you can take in the Japanese sunrise, standing at the crater's edge on the highest peak in the Land of the Rising Sun. It was described as 'unparalleled' and I was hooked. Sadly, I have no recollection of the sunrise or the crater. In fact, despite having been there, I couldn't pick out the summit of Mount Fuji in a volcano line up, but I know I was there because I have a photo of the sunrise. I didn't take it, but it's on my camera.

We got ourselves kitted out. I had hiking boots, mountain-worthy trousers, a fleece and various other 'essential' accoutrements (I'd clearly been one of those customers that made outdoor retailers rub their hands together in glee). John had some trainers, jeans, a jumper and a coat. When the day came, we got the bus to the fifth step, which is the bottom of the path at the edge of the forest and the place many people begin the zig-zag climb. My heart began to pound as we got closer, until I noticed the couples and even a family with young kids who got off the bus alongside us, had never heard of North Face or rapid moisture transfer and were mostly wearing casual clothes and loafers. I looked down at the young kid in his flip flops and smiled. Clearly this was going to be easier than I thought.

The shop at the fifth step was filled with mountain things as well as cheap plastic toys. We wandered around aimlessly until John found the cans of oxygen and decided he needed one. I laughed at him as he handed over his hard-earned money. It reminded me of the oxygen bar I'd stumbled into one day in Kyoto, where I lived. It stood at the side of a traditional Japanese cobbled street on the way up to Kiyomizu, the famous temple on stilts. I noticed the shop because to be honest you couldn't miss it. It stood out like a Jackson Pollock at a Michelangelo exhibition and enticed me in with its pretty blue strip lights. People were standing at intervals around the shop, attached to neon poles via face masks, sucking at the oxygen like cigarette addicts. It felt like being in a scene from the original Bladerunner, or some other kind of weird sci-fi movie, but then Japan often felt like that to me. I couldn't bring myself to pay the exorbitant fee for the oxygen that, as I understood it, was freely available outside the shop if you breathed deeply enough, so I left, the world around me ricocheting back 50 years as I stepped onto the cobbles.

When John picked up the can of oxygen in the shop at the bottom of Mt Fuji, it made sense that it would be more helpful at Fuji's 3,770 odd metres than the 1,000 metres the oxygen bar had over the sea level, but I knew I wouldn't be needing it. I'd recently spent five months living in La Paz, the capital city of Bolivia. The highest capital in the world, it rests at the bottom of a bowl in the Altiplano that could boast at being roughly the same height as the summit of Mt Fuji - if it wanted to, which it probably doesn't.

I'm not proud to admit that I was feeling smug. I'd managed to live at the equivalent height of Fuji's summit for a number of months, and despite typhoid, I'd survived. Therefore, I cleverly surmised, I would hardly need oxygen if I was only going to be at that height for a few hours. John however, had been living in the wilds of London and felt the need to pack oxygen in a can.

We started up what we had been told was the less busy track feeling strong, healthy and ready. Steering my mountain wear around the Japanese pottering along in their Saturday sweat pants, I looked up at the pathway looming above. It didn't look quite as easy from this vantage point, but the path was broad and easy going. Until it wasn't any more. Now the path had narrowed and was steeper as we edged past the strolling groups. Eager to get to the top, we didn't bother to stop at the first few rest huts for tea. As dusk closed in around us, John developed a case of mild diarrhoea, which spurred us on faster in a constant search for the next toilet shack.

By the time we stopped at a small cabin, it must have been about midnight, we were cold to the bone and ravenous. I looked around the hut, which was crowded in one corner with a pile of bodies sleeping like sardines in a can. Bodies, I noticed, that were wearing a lot more than they had been further down the mountain.

It struck me that they had cleverly brought extra clothes along and were layering up as they ascended. I, on the other hand, in all my flash mountain gear, had not brought any more layers and was shivering inside my bones as a result. John was also shivering, but he wasn't sure if it was because of the cold or his unfortunate bowel situation. We made our way to the side of the cabin without the bodies where a thin man in a cap and apron was serving steaming bowls of udon noodles. Having devoured them alongside a host of other slurping diners, we got up to leave. The man sitting on the opposite side of the bench stopped us, pointing at the pile of bodies and saying something in earnest. As between us, we had the combined Japanese ability of a 2 year old, we couldn't understand what he was saying, but it seemed pretty obvious that he wanted us to stay for a bit. I looked over, there was no more floor space and I didn't fancy squashing several Japanese people with my comparatively large surface area-ness, so I smiled and made exaggerated gestures to indicate that we weren't tired and were ready to get going. Another man stepped in and tried to take my small pack off, but we were keen to arrive at the top and wanted to rest at the hut there instead. I tousled myself free in the politest way I could and awkwardly secured my headlamp while John took another dash to the bathroom. The pack man was still telling me something incomprehensible when my mountain partner returned, but John wanted to get going to the next toilet and by this time loud sighs that clearly meant, 'shut up,' were drifting over from the pile of bodies. We excused ourselves by bowing and stepped out into the freezing air. Our headlamps shone bleakly through the mist as we climbed, the voices of the men in the hut fading into the distance.

"What do you think they were saying?" I asked John after some time in silence. He shrugged miserably. I could tell he wasn't up to conversation, so I left it there.

Mt Fuji was quiet. It wasn't the nothing kind of quiet you get in an empty room, it was more like the thick silence of something large that is definitely there but isn't making any sound. Space stretched out around her in all directions, filled with freezing darkness. Our lamps shone tiny circles of light on her narrow rocky path as we forged on, lost in thought. It was a while before one of us broke through the silence.

"Have you noticed it's just us now?"

I had noticed, but I didn't get to say so because at that moment the altitude sickness I knew I wasn't going to get hit me like a truck. It wiped the energy clean out of me in one swift whack and I hurled the udon I'd just consumed down the side of Mt Fuji.

"Want to turn back?" John asked.

"No, I just climbed too quickly after eating. It's probably what they were trying to say."

I continued to bless Mother Earth with the contents of my stomach at regular intervals as we clambered on. I could tell John wanted to hang back and be sympathetic, but his bowels were calling him forward to the next relief. I followed him miserably, failing to adhere to every piece of advice I'd ever been given about mountain sickness. My body slowed and faltered, but I was damned if I wasn't going to see that 'unparalleled' sunrise after all this. I'd be okay, I'd seen a kid climbing the same mountain for goodness sake.

I'd be fine as soon as we got to the summit and could rest, besides, down looked ominous in the blackness. I wondered whether Lady Parkes had had this trouble as she ran up, without the aid of breathable thermal underwear I imagine.

We hauled ourselves up some of the bigger boulders at the top, each one felt like a cliff face to me and as I crested the last one, I took a moment to consider how it would feel to have a group of enraged men on my tail at this moment in time. I saluted Parkes' courage. Then I threw up again.

Our excitement was palpable as we reached the top and the prospect of a warm, cosy hut to sleep until sunrise. But the hut wasn't there, or it wasn't open. Instead, a howling gale blasted us backwards in pitch black and we had to crouch down and crawl across the rocks to avoid being blown down the side. We crawled clumsily, unable to see whether we were near the crater or not until I found what looked like a small wall of rock in the dim light of my torch. I just couldn't believe there was nothing there! I'm sure we both wanted to say, 'Ohhhhh! that's what they were trying to tell us!' But neither of us had the capacity. There was nothing but blackness, a freezing windstorm and this tiny barrier of stones we were curled up behind.

John sidled off to find whatever piece of land felt appropriate to use as a toilet while I used the piece of land next to me to throw up some more. By the time he returned I was retching about once a minute. I heard him stagger over and collapse next to me, which I confess I thought was over dramatic for a case of the runs, even under these circumstances. Then I realised the sound I could hear under the wind was John shivering and trying unsuccessfully to breathe. He was gasping desperately for air as I lurched up in the manner of someone severely drunk and floundered around inside his pack with frozen, useless hands, hoping to grasp the can of oxygen. The one I had laughed at so smugly. Altitude sickness was making me awkward and slow, it seemed to take an age to lift the can and hand it to him. When I did, he took long gulps of pure oxygen while I threw up some more and tried to drink between bouts to get some water into my dehydrated body. As John's breathing capacity increased, mine decreased until I was the one gasping for breath. He held the can while I breathed for a moment and it sunk in that if we waited for sunrise like this, we weren't likely to be around to see it.

"We have to get down now!" John pulled at me as we crawled back to the path and began staggering down like two paralytic drunks, breathing in the style of two old men who'd smoked 60 a day for life and were in the end stages of emphysema. Not quite the majestic Mt Fuji experience I'd envisaged.

A way down, as I continued to hurl the contents of my stomach at frequent intervals, we came across the crowd that had been peacefully sleeping in the hut what seemed like so long ago now. Clearly this was the correct time to ascend for sunrise. The path was narrow up here, marked by a thin rope either side, usually enough for one line, going up or coming down I guess. Here we were messing things up by wanting to go down at the coming up time. It caused no end of logistical problems, which turned out to be nothing compared to the problems my stomach caused. I'd been trying to drink water as much as possible to replace everything I'd lost, and it was now coming out projectile fashion without warning. Each bout surprised me as much as the unsuspecting climbers who had to find the energy and space to leap sideways in an effort to avoid the line of fire. It was like a scene from the Exorcist on replay and there was nothing I could do but dab at my mouth and mutter, "Excuse me," each time.

As we returned to the seventh step at 2,700 metres, the frequency had lessened, and the sun was beginning to warm the day. I collapsed onto a bench, my head thumping and John, whose lungs were fully functioning again, called me to come and see the breathtaking array of colors streaking across the sky. But I was so busy groaning and trying not to be sick that I just couldn't bring myself to care. An alien craft could have been beaming me a personalised message across the heavens and I wouldn't have bothered to look. I handed John my camera.

"Take a photo will you," I murmured, "I'll look at it when we get back."

Retrospective top tips on how not to die on Mt Fuji:

- ↘ Don't risk any amount of smugness
- ↘ Take Oxygen in a can
- ↘ Try actually listening to advice on mountain sickness
- ↘ Do whatever the Japanese are doing

Lesson Learned

I don't always know best (damn it).

PANIC IN THE PAMPAS
The Amazon, Bolivia, 2000

Reasons for near-death:
Inexperienced guide on his first trip; Getting lost
in serpent infested waters; Possible implosion due
to infuriating Dutch man.

We sat on the branch of a tree in the middle of the bog. Soaked to the waist, I shivered and peered down at the murky water looking to see if there were more snakes waiting to get us. "I wish you'd been bitten," snarled Marten, the inconceivably unpleasant Dutch man, under his breath.

I didn't say anything because there didn't seem to be anything to say. Besides, his long, giraffe-like features meant he could have pushed me in from his place three people along the tree. Instead, I took pleasure in remembering his squeals as the mosquitoes had eaten him alive earlier that day. Charlotte moved the conversation on to more important things.

"Where are we?" She asked Angelo, our guide, who grinned widely.

"We are lost." He said confidently.

We had enthusiastically signed up for what promised to be an eco-friendly trip along the river into the heart of the Amazon pampas. Mario, our guide, produced himself at the small, dilapidated shop desk and began talking about the trip details, demonstrating his experience proficiently. It was to be a small group. Charlotte and I were joined by Heidee, a dark-haired South-African girl and Marten, a long-rather-than-tall Dutch man in his twenties who had various electrical gadgets slung around his torso and was wearing a large scowl.

We set off by minibus, Mario the guide chatting excitedly as he drove. A mixture of excitement and anticipation made us all chatty - except Marten, who was silent save the several moments he chose to open his window and yell random words in Spanish.

"MALO," he yelled at a surprised dog. Nobody said anything as he maneuvered his long frame back inside the bus. Minutes later he was out the window again, "RAPIDO," he screamed at the top of his large lungs in the direction of a bewildered family who were changing a tyre at the side of the road.

The rest of us exchanged sideways glances before continuing the conversation as if nothing had happened and the journey continued in much the same way until Mario swerved unexpectedly into a large gravel car park.

"Hold on," he swung himself out the door and trotted over to a lone, white minibus a few metres away. We waited patiently while animated voices floated out of the bus, blowing away in the wind before we could catch what they were saying. Eventually, a jeans-clad bottom emerged from the back door, shuffling out with difficulty until a young, nervous-looking guy in a worn t-shirt appeared. The bus sped away and he tentatively began walking towards us.

"Erm, where's Mario?" Charlotte ventured as he got into the driver's seat.

"I am trainee guide." The boy said, taking a deep breath and smiling big. "My name Angelo," he raised his voice above the growl of the engine as it choked to a start. "Almost qualified," he added reassuringly. No-one spoke while we all took some time to wonder what the hell was going on. Charlotte was first to recover.

"What happened to Mario?"

"He sick."

"He didn't seem sick," said Heidee frowning.

"Problem with nose," he pointed to his nose to demonstrate

the source of Mario's dumping us and nodded wisely. An air of distinct uneasiness drifted around the bus.

"How old are you?" Marten demanded after too long in silence.

"Angelo is 19." He looked round at us all, grinning widely and narrowly missing a head on collision at the same time.

"Have you done this before?" I offered.

"No, first time," he grinned.

When we arrived at the river, Charlotte, Heidee and I had a hurried discussion about whether it was wise to continue given the circumstances while Marten helped our guide get the handmade wooden longboat ready and piled his electrical equipment up one end. We decided to continue on the grounds that a) we were now in the middle of nowhere and b) we had already paid.

Angelo was looking suspiciously at the electronics when we got to the river's edge.

"We need space for people in boat," he ventured.

"I'm not moving my stuff," growled Marten and he sat down amongst his treasure.

We spaced ourselves and our packs along the rest of the boat and peace washed over us as we glided silently through the thick forest to our camp, an hour down river.

The camp consisted of a hammock and some mosquito nets set at the side of the bank. A short walk through the forest, watching for any man-eating spiders, was a hole known to some as a toilet. About fifteen foot from the hole, a giant sleeping alligator (which I think is actually a black caiman) had set up home. I ran to get Angelo and pointed at the large dinosaur.

"Not worry. He not fast on land." Angelo informed us. "Always go to toilet in pairs. One watch him, one do toilet. If he move, run."

This trip was going to take a lot of trust.

The next few days were incredible. We woke at dawn to the songs of the amazon, the healthy, crisp air expanding our lungs as we emerged from beneath our mosquito nets. Angelo took us along the river pointing out animals I'd only dreamt of seeing in person. Sloths dangled confidently from high branches, huge piles of turtles balanced in pyramid structures rising from the water, while howler monkeys screeched in the canopy above us. I felt as though the Amazon was somehow cleaning me from the inside out. We swam with the most beautiful pink dolphins praying it was true that piranha don't come near the dolphins for fear of being eaten. I use the term 'swim' loosely because I can't actually swim, so Heidee, Marten and Angelo swam while I flapped, trying to stay afloat. Mostly though, I demanded that Charlotte, who'd stayed in the boat, give me a blow by blow account of the whereabouts of an alligator whose eyes were watching our every move from the other side of the river.

We grew to like our enthusiastic young guide, but it is hard to fully trust someone who continually asks if they are doing okay.

Marten and his electrical appliances weren't happy. They didn't like the magic of gliding along the river at dawn in a hand-crafted longboat because it was too slow.

"Why don't you get an engine?" He growled, unwinding the straps of his camera and video equipment. Angelo didn't know how to answer and chose to point out some capybara playing on the bank instead.

"Seen them." He complained. "We do the same thing every day."

After that, he channelled his boredom into pointing out the similarity between certain tree trunks and parts of the female anatomy, which he filmed or took photos of to prove his point, laughing lasciviously as he did until I noticed I felt safer with the alligator and piranha than I did with him.

The next morning, we woke to more than the music of the Amazon. Above the usual chirping, the odd screech and the buzzing hum of the forest was the sound of someone cursing and repeatedly slapping their head.

Marten had insisted on sleeping outside in the hammock despite our young guide's fervent attempts to dissuade him, ("Don't tell me what to do."). Charlotte and I exchanged winces as Marten turned around to reveal huge hammock-shaped wheels indented along one side of his head where insects had been feasting all night.

Between them, swollen pieces of face burst out in nasty looking crimson diamonds.

"Damn mosquitoes," he wailed, flailing his arms and thumping his face. Charlotte, who had taken part in many an argument with Marten, filled with a moment of compassion and went to get some cream, then offered to put it on for him.

"Get away from me." He bit wildly. The alligator around the corner seemed like the friendlier option.

Breakfast was awkward, and a heavy silence lay across our camp whilst the natural world continued to fill the air with animated life, dancing easily through the tension. Angelo tried his best to placate Marten by telling him about our day. We were to go on a walk in the pampas later, looking for anaconda and other wildlife.

"Is it safe?" Heidee ventured.

"I will have machete!" Angelo grinned and held up a broad silver knife. Then stage-whispered to Charlotte, his chosen confidante, "I am doing okay yes?"

I sucked on my watermelon and wondered how much Angelo's machete would help us in the event of say... a three-pronged alligator attack, while Marten vociferously informed the forest that he hoped an anaconda would eat Charlotte for lunch.

That morning, we didn't see so many animals on our river jaunt, which wasn't surprising as the grunting and slapping and moaning sounds coming from our boat would have scared Freddie Kruger away. Marten flailed his unfathomably large hands around and swore in vain attempts to protect his mosquito bites that seemed to be attracting more insects while the rest of us tried to pretend we weren't a little happy that the jungle was dishing out its own form of justice. I swear a dolphin winked at me as the boat rocked from side to side.

Later that morning, our pampas walk began. Angelo swiped at the long grass with his machete, carving a path for us. We stopped at a cow skeleton while he told us of the serpent that probably killed it.

"Serpent kill cow very quick. One bite," he said with glee, and did an impression of what I think was meant to be a snake biting a cow. A few minutes later he suddenly stopped his wild pampas chopping. "Shhh. Hear that?"

We stopped dead, listening to the strange sound.

"It is song of serpent. There are many here. If bite you, one hour to live."

Seeing as we had been walking for more than an hour, and the minibus was a further hour or so upriver there didn't seem to be much hope of finding help before the sands of time ran out. As we walked on, I felt fear rising inside me like steam from an underground vent. On he chopped and on we walked until we were wading, knee deep, in a bog and Heidee spotted serpents swimming around our feet. All our fears merged instantly creating a surge of chaos. Angelo panicked and told us to get out of the water immediately. Charlotte was shouting at him, "You're the guide, you get us out NOW." Meanwhile Heidee grabbed Angelo and refused to let go of him, making it almost impossible for him to move. I tried to run, got my foot stuck in the mud at the bottom of the bog and fell over into the serpent infested waters. Marten meanwhile, whose filming of parrots flying overhead had been interrupted screamed a frighteningly detailed threat about spraying pepper spray in Heidee's face.

The serpents continued to zip carefree around the bog while we scuttled over to the tree conveniently placed in the middle and climbed up to safety.

It was then that Angelo happily informed us that we were lost.

I would love to say that we used our internal compasses to make our way back to the camp, or that Angelo had a flash of inspiration and remembered his training enough to lead us in the right direction. Sadly, it wasn't like this. We listened to Angelo wondering aloud which direction we should try and pondering on whether he recognized a certain bush or not until the light began to fade. Marten remembered his new GPS contraption and led us back through the bog and the pampas, past the cow skeleton to the spurious comfort of our river camp and the mosquito nets to hide under. I was simultaneously grateful to him for saving us and annoyed that it was he who had saved us.

That night, as I curled up sleepily under my net. I heard the call of the serpent close by, the one Angelo had made us listen to in the pampas - the one that belonged to the snake that killed the cow in a single bite. I froze, wondering just how close it was then tucked the edges of my net in to prevent any breach of security and attempted to maneuver my limbs into positions that made them hard for serpents to get their teeth into. Finally, after several hours of fretting, I managed to convince myself that if it were my destiny to be bitten by a serpent, then so be it. If it wasn't, I'd be best off getting some sleep before the morning and another day of dealing with Marten.

Retrospective top tips on how not to die in the Amazon:

- ↘ *If your promised guide disappears half-way there due to a 'nose problem', don't continue*
- ↘ *Always go to the toilet in twos*
- ↘ *Don't trust a guide who continuously asks you if he is doing okay*

Lesson Learned

That person really annoying me could have something vital to share.

SNAKE ON A RAFT
Northern Thailand, 2000

Reasons for near-death:
Cocky young guide showing off; Angry snake bent on revenge.

    If you're thinking of getting run over then Bangkok is definitely the place for you. If the car you're aiming for misses you, don't worry because a passing motorbike or tuk-tuk is bound to take you out. Within a few days of arriving, I had worked out the key to surviving the traffic while getting across to the side of the road I wanted. The trick is to launch yourself confidently into the path of the oncoming traffic and hope. Occasionally they slow down, but more often will career into another lane of traffic and use their horns to sort things out between themselves, leaving you free to run for your life.

The Koh San Road is a fascinating place, though it gets old quickly. Designed exclusively for backpackers, within the scope of about 10 metres you can choose between a hand-tailored suit, a fake ID or a rare copy of a book from about 1936. At least you could back in 2000. And if you aren't after any of the above, you can amuse yourself getting conned by the men who wait outside the temples down the road to inform you that all the places you are going to visit happen to be closed today and there is only one place open and he happens to be free to take you there (for a fee)... and on the way why don't you stop at a good shop he knows? Yes, it's his friend's shop but there is nothing else open! They aren't threatening and I discovered will happily play along while you point out all the temples on your map.

"Is this one open?" *points to temple on map

"Closed."

"This one? And this one?" *more pointing

"Closed madam."

"How about these ones?"

"All closed," he grins.

"Even this one?"

This was the stage at which they usually disappeared to look for someone who didn't point to all the temples on the map.

The wilds of Bangkok get a bit much after a few days so when my friend Charlotte arrived, we traveled up to the forests of Northern Thailand to get a different taste of the country. Despite the commotion of the capital, Thailand has a peaceful feeling to it. Every country has an undercurrent of energy as unique as a signature and Thailand's is very gentle. The people generally have a kind and friendly quality about them, even when they are telling you every-thing is closed. Further North, the forests add clarity and richness to the experience.

We were camping in a village and amusing the locals by screeching when various insects descended on us. A praying mantis landing across your face is a screech-worthy offense in my opinion but once we'd found a snake in our bed that it took three men to carefully capture between them, I felt the praying mantis hadn't been so bad after all.

The following day, we stood on the riverbank as the guides we had hired to take us upriver finished making two long bamboo rafts. We were on the second raft as we pushed off from the bank. The youthful guide stood at the front using a lofty bamboo culm to punt us through the muddy waters. I stood warily a few feet behind him, Charlotte behind me and another girl at the back, spaced out evenly to ensure optimum balance.

In silence, we listened to the satisfying swoosh of water each time he heaved the pole out hand over hand until it rose above him awkwardly. The second it looked as though he was going to lose it, he would plunge it confidently back into the river bed to propel us along.

The trees lining the river exhaled their vibrant energy, which hung on the air, so each breath tasted of fresh emerald forest. It was divine calm drifting along the river.

Then the guide started to show off. He turned and grinned.

"Watch this." He heaved his pole out of the water, hands working fast until it was free and he could lift it high in the air where it swayed ominously.

"See snake sleep in tree." He waved the pole at a tree overhanging the river high above us. A snake was coiled in its branches enjoying the sun. We smiled and pointed it out to each other, then he took his pole and whacked wildly at the tree until the long reptile squirmed, slithered and finally fell clumsily through the air, landing with a smack on the water's surface. He laughed loudly.

"Hey! Why did you do that?" Charlotte yelled angrily from behind me, but the guide didn't answer because the snake, understandably enraged, was thrashing around the edge of our raft trying to board it. The guide tried to look cool while he poked at it with his staff, trying his best to prevent it from clambering onto the bamboo. He prodded and flipped it, but it was some time before he could get the pole under the middle of the snake, so it didn't slip off. Then he hooked it into the air and hurled it away. It landed neatly on the raft in front of us and slid into the water, much to the surprise of the other guide. We watched the scene replay almost exactly as the snake tried to mount their raft. Finally, that guide managed to hook and flip it. The poor creature found himself flying through the air a third time until he came down on the water with a thud, floating motionless before disappearing below the surface. I stared as the green hue blurred and sank into the murk. Snakes weren't my favourite things, but I couldn't bear to see it die unnecessarily.

Our young guide grinned the brazen yet clearly relieved grin of someone recently released from a death sentence.

"Exciting!" He offered before turning back to his task. But it wasn't exciting, it was horrible, and I could no longer feel the peace and the forest air. I turned to make a, 'What did he think he was doing?!' face at Charlotte and found a look of absolute horror on hers.

"It's okay, it's gone now," I reassured her. She shook her head. "Don't worry..." I started, but I didn't finish.

"It's behind you," she screamed, and I flew around to see the snake was alive and well and had not only made it back to our raft but had somehow gotten onto it and was currently rearing up, neck waving, tongue flicking and hissing as it jabbed wildly at the air in front of me.

If you google, 'Are snakes vengeful?' you'll find several experts telling you that they aren't and that the idea of snakes seeking revenge is a myth. The more I travel though, the more I find it is best not to make assumptions, even if said presumption is based on expertise. I have learned it is more beneficial to take what is happening as it comes and go with what's in front of you instead of what is in your head. What was in front of me at that moment was a vengeful snake. So I did what any decent, wise, person would do and backed slowly and calmly away.

I wish.

What I actually did was to scream and dart behind Charlotte using her as a shield and (she claims) pushed her forwards hoping the snake would get her instead of me. I guess I'm not quite the friend I thought I was. In my defense, I have no memory of doing it and was therefore acting under trauma. Thankfully, the snake that shouldn't have had the capacity to return to seek revenge, not only wanted revenge, he wanted to direct his anger towards exactly the right person. We stood motionless as the snake hissed and weaved its head as if looking for something. Then, it turned to the guide behind and immediately attacked.

The commotion that ensued was terrifying. The previously boastful guide panicked as he dodged the snake's angry attacks while pulling the elongated pole out of the water as fast as he could in order to defend himself. It seemed longer this time. Meanwhile, as Charlotte and I had backed away as far as we could and were now at the end with the other girl, we were dangerously unbalanced. The front of the raft lifted out of the water, causing the snake and the guide to slide down the sloping bamboo towards us. The snake hissed fiercely and thrashed as the guide flailed at it with the pole, shouting in Thai. The lengthy beam he had was sturdy in water but ridiculously treacherous to control out of it. Everyone was screeching now, including the people on the other raft and the young guide fighting for his life on the end of our airborne raft. Our feet were underwater, and we inched forward toward the fight tentatively, in an effort to stabilise the bamboo. Just as we did, the guide managed to wrap the snake around the pole enough to fling it upwards once more.

It spun through the air far into the distance and against all odds, landed on the only other raft on the water. An old Thai man, out for a peaceful drift on his raft, got the shock of his life when a snake flew out of the sky, lashing out at him as it thudded on the hollow wood. We watched in stunned silence as the old man and the snake thrashed around wildly until finally, they came to a stop and the snake slopped into the water. The man turned and continued on his way as if nothing had happened.

I spent the rest of the trip checking all sides and ends of the raft just in case.

Retrospective top tips on how not to die when faced with deadly snake on a raft:

- ↘ *Don't believe everything google says*
- ↘ *Never trust a cocky guide*
- ↘ *Hiding behind a friend works - but I don't recommend it*

Lesson Learned

I can never say how I would react to something until it's happened to me.

HECTOR FRANCISCO AND THE MISSING VILLAGE
Machu Picchu, Peru 2000

Reasons for (almost-but-not-quite) near-death:
Hiring a guide who turned out to not be a guide;
listening to the non-guide's advice.

I was still traveling with Charlotte when I went to Peru. She'd forgiven me for using her as a shield during the snake incident in Thailand and we'd since managed to survive several other countries together. We took the bus from Bolivia, stopping off at Lake Titicaca to visit the birthplace of the sun on the way from La Paz to Cuzco. Bus journeys weren't so bad for me because (provided they weren't on windy roads when I would instantly throw up) I had an uncanny ability to fall asleep the second I sat down - if I was lucky enough to have the window seat. The aisle seat was a different matter. Every bus was filled to capacity, over capacity to be accurate. Each passenger, having climbed up and tied to the roof more bulging sacks than it should be possible to carry, would squash their way down the aisle to settle in with about fifty other standing passengers. Some carried babies, others parrots, or maybe a table, but all managed to fit into spaces that defied the laws of physics. This means that seated passengers who get on first will run for the window seat, as Charlotte and I often did. She usually won simply because she could argue well and put forward viable points about the fact that I was wasting the views from the window seat due to my prolonged sleeping. Whoever ended up in the aisle seat (me) could look forward to being sat on by different sized, shaped and smelling people. Or babies. Or animals. Or furniture. The day we traveled to Peru, my companion felt sorry for me and gave me the window. I was delighted. I watched the scenery bounce by and marvelled at the range of luggage on the roof of the bus next to us.

"Is that what I think it is?" I asked Charlotte. She leaned on me and peered out at the roof.

"A cow's head." She pointed out. It was bouncing up and down between a cloth bag and a chair, apparently not attached to a body any more.

"Oh." I said. "I thought so," and promptly fell asleep. When I woke, Charlotte had disappeared and in her place were the largest pair of bosoms I had ever come across. One eye peered out from a small gap in the middle. It appeared to be saying, "Help," but I was too busy laughing to be of assistance. Besides, there was nowhere else for the bosoms to go.

We stopped and the driver went to get a drink. I was desperate to go to the toilet. A long line of people were waiting, with their extensive luggage, to board the bus. I stood in the doorway and asked the nearest few in my best Spanish where the toilet was. They laughed as they pointed out the fact that I was standing next to one on the bus. I laughed with them, turning red as I did and opened the door to the foul-smelling room. I needed the toilet so badly, I didn't care about the smell. Besides, I'd been in worse toilets on UK buses. I heaved a sigh of relief as I let go of several bottles of water I'd consumed earlier that day and emerged from the toilet to a raucous commotion going on outside. I peered out to see people shouting and veering off in different directions, desperately trying to grab their luggage in an attempt to avoid the huge puddle making its way from the bottom of the bus down the line. A warm dismay washed over me as I realised what they were trying to avoid. I had no idea the toilet didn't have a bottom to it! Someone pointed at me and shouted something I didn't understand. I muttered a quick, "Lo siento," and went off in search of biscuits. What else could I do?

Charlotte relinquished all responsibility for me on my return, so I comforted myself by falling asleep.

Cuzco is the charming city I woke up to. We disembarked and found ourselves somewhere to stay by taking a chance and following one of the touts at the bus station. Two of Charlotte's friends were meeting us here and after a couple of days for them to acclimatise, we were to trek to Machu Picchu together. We sat in a local bar and planned for our Andean hike over a few beers. At this time, it was possible to trek the route to the ancient ruins without joining a tour. We didn't want to have to travel in a large group, but didn't want to leave everything to chance either and decided to hire our own guide. Charlotte's friends weren't great in the Spanish department and Charlotte and I hadn't gotten that much further than the detailed weather conversations we'd learned at our home study in Cochabamba, but four bad speakers are better than one - aren't they? When we went to the travel shop at the edge of Cuzco, they assured us in bad English that the guide we had paid them for would meet us at KM 82, the start of the trek. He would have his own food for the four-day hike over the mountains. We checked in bad Spanish that he knew the way and would have his own tent and they confirmed this, assuring us that Hector spoke English and would be the perfect guide. Now we needed tents and food for us. None of us wanted to carry too much for the roughly 82 kilometres we would be walking. We knew it would be lots of up and lots of down, followed by a lot more up several times and so we packed the minimum we thought we could get by on.

When we arrived at KM82 there were various men milling around, presumably all guides. One of them came running over to us.

"I am guide." He said smiling.

"The one we booked?"

"Yes, yes! You are…"

"Charlotte and Amanda."

"Yes! Good." He said. "Let's go."

"You're Hector?" I wasn't sure.

"Yes yes, good. We go."

And off we went. Climbing through the sacred valley. Hector pointed out incredible Inca ruins and proudly showed us the Cusichaca River as we walked. At lunch, he nipped off to talk to one of the other guides and it took us until the afternoon to realise that Hector's English was about as good as our Spanish. It wasn't until the evening though, that we realised Hector didn't have a tent with him. Or any food. His small backpack was housing a bottle of home-made Cocoroco, which is 96% ethanol, and a spare t-shirt. How did we not notice his lack of provisions before? After a long conversation in which we tried to understand each other as we explained the man in the shop had said Hector would have his own tent and food, and Hector appeared to insist that he never did, we realised we weren't getting anywhere and moved on to find a tour group and ask the guides from there if they had room in their tent for one more. Thankfully they did as the two-man tents we had hired were fit for 1.5 children and wouldn't have managed a Hector as well. We shared our meagre dinner and breakfast rations with him, attempting conversation that never really got going and watching in disbelief as Hector managed to take gulps of his 96% alcohol without coughing his guts up.

The night was cold, but the sky was perfect. I peeked out of the tent to find a galaxy of the brightest stars smiling at me from a clear indigo background. "You're doing it!" They shouted. "This is what you've always wanted."

The next day was hell. I hated it because I couldn't breathe. The further we climbed the harder it was to get enough breath into my struggling lungs. I was way behind the others when Hector appeared.

"Problem?" he asked.

"It's my breathing." I tried to show him how short my breaths were and sat down, utterly exhausted. Hector fished around in his tiny backpack and pulled out the bottle.

"I can't drink that!" I protested, waving my arms and shaking my head to make sure he understood.

"No drink. Sniff," he laughed and took a big sniff from the bottle to show me.

What good could a sniff do! But I had no other ideas or offers of help, so I sniffed. A big sniff like Hector had advised.

The fumes ripped through my lungs, making channels where there weren't any and burning my insides. I coughed one of my lungs up but when I stood upright, my breathing was easier.

"Again," he encouraged.

Three long sniffs later and I was able to breathe and walk at the same time. Hector walked with me for a while sipping at the poisonous liquid and grinning until we caught the others up at the 4,200 metre summit. The Andean mountains spread out before us in all their glory, which was lucky as we had realised we didn't really have enough food for us, much less us and Hector. We basked in the sun and the view of lush green peaks as we shared our packet sausage and mash with him for lunch. I was grateful to our guide for saving my lungs, even if he'd done it by burning holes in them.

That night, after a feast of potato goop, Hector went off to share a tent with some other guides.

The following day, we realised we weren't just short of food, we actually didn't have enough left to feed ourselves and Hector. Paul was blessed with diarrhoea, which is not easy to deal with on a busy path through the Andes, and the path was busy that day, ancient Inca steps leading us all on to the promise of an experience to treasure. I remembered Mrs Joseph telling me about enjoying journeys not just destinations but the thought of seeing this magical place was the only thing keeping me going. My legs and lungs seemed not to like journeys as much as destinations and I found myself longing for Hector and his toxic fumes, but Hector was not happy for a reason we didn't know. We hadn't even told him about the lack of food yet. Other guides were pointing out Inca buildings along the way, ours was nowhere to be seen. It was just when I believed I couldn't go on that a tall, American man appeared beside me.

"You suffer from altitude-induced asthma," he drawled.

"I'm not sure." I ventured, frowning.

"It wasn't a question," he smiled. "I have seen it before. Try using the rest-step." And he showed me how to walk up steps ensuring I straightened each leg and paused at the end of a step. Then he disappeared.

I used his method for the rest of the trek. It was a miracle. It seemed slower, but I found I didn't need breaks as much as the others, and I was breathing okay. Hector turned up just as dusk was sweeping across the mountains. Charlotte and Paul had negotiated him dinner as well as space in a tent and we were looking forward to what little food we had when he shocked us all by refusing point blank to sleep or eat with the other guides.

"But we don't have enough food, and they do."

"My friend will cook for all in village. Close by!" he exclaimed. "He very good cook."

"Are you sure?" We looked at the map. "There's no mention of a village here."

"Small village. I am sure." He nodded firmly and began walking. We looked at each other for a while until his figure was disappearing in the growing mist, then picked up our backpacks and followed. I couldn't help looking forward to some real food in a village.

The red sun dipped below the lush mountains and valleys and on we walked, following the figure ahead. Charlotte called out.

"It's almost dark. Where's the village, Hector?"

"Over next hill," he pointed. "No worry. Somewhere to sleep."

My body heaved a sigh of relief. And we walked on. And on.

By the time dusk had moved on to darkness we started to panic. The other hiking groups were far behind and it would be ridiculously dangerous to try getting back there in the dark. But Hector continually reassured us. Finally, he stopped and turned to look at us.

"Are we here?"

He nodded unconvincingly.

This was it? We caught up with him expectantly and peered through the darkness. With my torch I could just make out a small, round pond in a clearing and…that was it. There was nothing else. This was the kind of village that didn't exist. We stood in stunned silence, listening to the sound of each other's hearts sinking. No village, no friend, no food, no shelter, no people. Nothing. What the hell were we going to do? There was no way back and we couldn't go on in the dark. My hands were stiff with cold and my face was starting to hurt, we were at high-altitude in the Andes with not enough food, water, shelter or fuel to see us through to Machu Picchu.

"Why would you do this?" I ventured in disbelief. Hector shrugged his shoulders.

Charlotte's friend started to freak out, pointing out the severity of our predicament and how she felt about it in no uncertain terms, shouts that cracked the frozen air like a pickaxe on ice. Her boy-friend tried to calm her down while we stood and wondered what to do.

If there was ever a time to test Mrs Joseph's theory, this was it. The frosty, wind-whipped Andean mountains didn't care about our plight so while Hector stood looking sulkily at the pond, Charlotte and I tried to stay calm and figure out how to divide one sausage into five and make Hector a warm shelter using a piece of string and some empty smash packets.

That was the moment something turned up - in the form of Pete and Julie from the Lake District. They emerged from the shadows and, with the enthusiasm of a couple of veteran scout leaders, informed us that they just happened to have spare food and fuel on them. They also happened to be trained in survival and after cooking us all a meal, fashioned a warm shelter for Hector to sleep in. Spanish was one of their languages (of course) and after speaking exuberantly with Hector for a while, they politely let us know that his name was Francisco and that he didn't like us. To be honest, we didn't like him either at this moment in time.

"You're not Hector?" Charlotte was incredulous. But Hector/ Francisco refused to speak to us. I wondered whether the real Hector was still waiting for us at Km 82.

The night was long and cold, it was windy up there, but thanks to our Angels of the North we survived. Francisco tried to make off with Pete and Julie the next day and we didn't see much more of him until we arrived at the ruins when he turned up to say, "Now you can give me a big tip," which we did. Then he said, "Tomorrow you will give me a big present," which we didn't. He said a sullen goodbye making off with two pairs of Charlotte's socks and a pair of her gloves.

It had all been worth it despite the guide who wasn't a guide. The final morning, we walked in the moonlight from 5am to catch the first rays of sun as they rise to shine through the gap between two mountains, lighting up the ancient city but leaving the surrounding area untouched. It was magical, ethereal. I felt as though I was watching something through a veil into another dimension. As I made my way towards the time-honored stone, cut majestically into the mountains, the arguments we'd had on the way, the dramatic turmoil and challenges of the last few days inexplicably disappeared. It was as if I'd walked through an invisible doorway that wiped them from me. I was left only with a warm glow and a feeling of deep peace.

Francisco must have known this happens, because it was soon after this that he came to ask for his tip.

Retrospective top tips on how not to die trekking to Machu Picchu:

- ⇲ *Endeavour to learn some Spanish other than the weather*
- ⇲ *Check your guide is actually your guide*
- ⇲ *Get yourself a good pair of lungs - or some 96% alcohol*
- ⇲ *Try bringing enough food and fuel*

Lesson Learned

Exactly what I need turns up exactly when I need it - even if I'm up a mountain in the dark in the middle of nowhere.

TEAR GAS, TYPHOID AND
THE GOOD DOCTOR
La Paz, Bolivia, 2000

Reasons for near-death:
Typhoid; Salmonella x2.

I was trying to convey to the long-suffering woman behind the airport counter that my backpack had not come through on the conveyer belt. My Spanish wasn't really up to it because there was no sun, rain, heat, cold, bus tickets or toilets involved, and they were my specialist subjects. I was tired and emotional. Charlotte had left for the UK at Lima airport and I had flown back to La Paz where I was to volunteer in an orphanage for a few months. I was apprehensive about finding a place to live and starting a new adventure alone again. Now I'd lost my backpack - or the airline had, and I was annoyed. I was trying to express my exasperation via body language and tone as the airline staff searched for my pack, when I noticed something was wrong. I looked around me, slowly taking in my surroundings. The airport wasn't like this last time I'd been there. Something was definitely amiss, but what was it? People bustled around me.

I hastily made my way back to the small counter by the conveyer belt.

"This is La Paz isn't it? I enquired.

The woman looked up in horror and rattled off a lot of Spanish words in quick succession, but the only one I understood was Chile.

"Chile? I'm in Chile?"

She nodded, ran out from behind the counter and grabbed my wrist, pulling me towards the doors I'd come through when I got off the plane.

"Vamos!" She yelled as she dragged me outside, then, because I was too slow, let go of my arm and pegged it across the tarmac to the small passenger plane I'd disembarked from, which was now taxiing across the runway to take off again.

"Stop!" She screeched in Spanish waving her arms in an attempt to hold up the plane. "Stop!"

I wasn't sure what struck me most, seeing her trying to flag down an airplane or watching her sprint across the tarmac in heels. I ran after her, unsure about the wisdom of hailing a plane in such a fashion, but she was determined and headed it off as it turned until she was facing the oncoming aircraft screaming and waving at the pilot, in breach of about 50 health and safety rules they didn't have in Chile.

The plane stopped. The door opened and a flight attendant appeared. The lady from the airline counter shouted animatedly up at her until she turned to beckon at me. A flight of stairs on wheels was hurriedly brought over and I climbed back up to the plane I should never have left muttering, "Lo siento," many times as I made my way past the alarmed passengers to my seat. I'd totally forgotten we were making a stop before arriving in Bolivia and to allay my embarrassment pretended to be asleep for the rest of the flight. When we arrived in La Paz, I waited until the end to climb back down the stairs and into the small terminal.

It was definitely the right airport this time. Only in La Paz, at just over 4,000 meters do you see newly arrived passengers staggering like drunks and dragging their luggage along the floor because they don't have the energy to pick it up.

Coca leaves are key. Altitude sickness makes the first week in La Paz feel like you've permanently just done a marathon you didn't train for and you don't know whether to throw up or lie down as a result. Coca leaves in hot water make some of the moments bearable. Chewing coca leaves isn't something I recommend unless you want a mouth full of soggy leaves, they taste exactly the way you imagine they would. Once you've been there for a while and got yourself some extra red blood cells, you're good to go.

La Paz is one of the most beautiful cities in the world in my opinion. It spreads from the altiplano down the side of the canyon to the city center at the bottom and up the other side. At night, the lights from the colored houses lining the canyon shine through the darkness like stars, guarded from above by the imposing Illimani, the highest mountain in the Cordillera Real at 6,438 meters.

I found myself a room in a house in Soparachi, a little way up the canyon from the main street and got my bearings. I explored the witches market, wandered the streets watching the indigenous ladies in their bowler hats and large skirts at the market stalls and got myself a Spanish teacher so I could communicate with the kids at the orphanage better. Charlotte and I had taken Spanish lessons when we'd first arrived in Bolivia. We had stayed with a family in Cochabamba for two weeks of intensive lessons with a lovely teacher called Betty. Our host, Feli, and her family claimed not to speak English, and as we were complete Spanish beginners mealtimes were a little trying. Breakfast consisted of lots of, "Esta frio!"

"Si frio."

Because it was. Luckily, by lunchtime it always heated up considerably, so we could try, "Tengo calor,"

"Tienes calor?"

"Si, tengo calor."

Which felt rich in depth and variety.

Feli started watching TV during mealtimes once she'd had enough of acknowledging the temperature. Tres Mujeres was her favorite, it was about three women who were inconceivably bad. We knew that because she would point every time one of them appeared on the screen and say, "Mal, muy mal," shaking her head as she did so. We would nod and mutter, "Si, muy mal," until we had finished eating. As our lessons progressed, we still struggled to say the simplest sentences. Neither of us had an aptitude for language, besides, our teacher was so lovely that we wanted to chat with her and found much of our lessons taken up with discussions, in English. There was a recent local news story in which a python was found in the Amazon with what looked suspiciously like a whole person inside him. Then Betty wanted to know what marmite was, plus she had a fascination with the word, 'crap,' and wanted to know how to use it correctly in English, which is something it takes time to explain. These important subjects hampered our Spanish learning and frustrated our hosts who still couldn't speak to us after our lessons. One lunchtime, Charlotte made a special effort to speak to Feli. She struggled and stuttered her way through a whole sentence in Spanish. I sat next to her, willing her on, trying to work out what the next word should be until she finished with a triumphant smile. We looked up to see Feli disappearing out the door. It was disappointing. We didn't get much better after that and got by mainly on gesticulation and random vocabulary so, now on my own, I was determined to try again.

My new Spanish teacher in La Paz was Maria. She was wonderful. She lived near the center of town and was one of the founder members of the human rights movement there in 1974. The first thing she did was to teach me how to honor the earth - pachamama - by pouring a little of whatever I drank on the earth before consuming it. I did learn some Spanish with her, but my desire to learn about her history and the movement she had started in the 70s meant my improvement was minimal. Besides, this was about the time I started throwing up at random. It happened a few times as I was walking the quiet backstreets to her house. Sometimes I'd throw up on the way to the orphanage too, but it seemed to be quick and I felt fine once it was over, so I didn't really worry about it. I'd gotten used to bowel problems in India and I'd never fully dispensed with the giardia I had in Nepal. It's amazing how you can become accustomed to these things and I didn't really notice them any more. When I started throwing up at random, I put it down to the change in food and the altitude. Then one day I threw up on myself while I was talking to Maria about the protests going on in La Paz. It started with a cough, which turned into loud guttural belching until I was retching like a cat with a stubborn hairball. Maria looked surprised, then concerned, then briefly annoyed before finding compassion and helping me clean up. She thought perhaps I should go and get checked out. I should have, but I wasn't sure which doctor to trust. I'd heard horror stories about some of the doctors in La Paz and I was I waiting to be sure which one was the best when the sickness seemed to get better.

I started working as an English teacher some evenings and made new friends who commented on the fact that I was losing weight. It was hard to cook properly at this altitude, I complained, the boiling point was all wrong and things didn't taste the same, so I took to eating cheap meals from the market stalls along the road. The coca farmers' protests were in full swing and they would fill the main street between the stalls daily, peacefully holding up signs and bustling around chatting and smoking. On my way to the orphanage, I had to wend my way through the chanting crowds, who Maria had told me were fighting for their lives. They were farmers whose livelihood had become illegal because the USA had made deals with the government to shut down the coca farms. The Americans had provided money as compensation for the farmers she told me, but the corrupt Bolivian government members had taken the money for themselves. The farmers had been stripped of their livelihood, their homes, their farms and their dignity in a matter of months. I never felt threatened as I walked among them, until the day the police decided the nasty, peaceful protesting should stop and began to intervene. From that day on, a hail of rubber bullets would occasionally start ricocheting into the crowds or canisters of tear gas would fly through the air. Some days, parts of the city were shrouded in smoke. It was a strange experience to be caught in the tear gas, particularly because the Bolivians seemed to accept it completely as part of the situation. It usually followed a pattern. I would be walking along, enjoying the atmosphere and smiling at the stallholders I saw every day, when suddenly, they would shout and franticly close up their wooden stalls while people around them would fall to the ground choking and spluttering. I don't know how, but they managed to close up every time before succumbing to the gas. I only got caught in the thick of it a couple of times, but it was a strange experience. My eyes and nose streamed and burned as I fell to the ground gasping. I would try to find clear air, sucking just above the cracks of the sidewalk, but couldn't catch my breath no matter how hard I tried. It stung at my lungs. The Bolivians always lit cigarettes at this point and passed them around. "It helps the oxygen go in," one told me as he handed me the cigarette. I hated smoking, but I took the tobacco stick and sucked at it, my face inches from the floor. They were right, somehow smoke seemed to get through and let some oxygen in too. We would lie on the floor in circles, passing the cigarette around until the gas cleared. Then, quick as a flash, normal life would resume. The indigenous women would rise majestically and open their stalls, the protesters picked up their signs and I would get up, tissue planted across my face and continue on my way to the orphanage.

As horrific as this was, I couldn't help enjoying the connection that happened during those times on the floor with the indigenous people of the country I had grown to love so much.

The throwing up started again, this time more frequently and more vigorously. I was finding it increasingly difficult to walk up the hill to the orphanage and I didn't have the patience I usually would for my English student, who kept offering to pay me to show her the exam paper.

"I give you 2 Bolivianos, you show me exam teacher yes?"

"No."

"Why teacher why?"

Having failed to pay me before the exam, she approached me again afterwards to see if I was more partial to increasing her score retrospectively.

"4 Bolivianos? 5?"

But I had already disappeared to the toilet where my body seemed to be ridding itself of every ounce of liquid it had ever ingested.

Perhaps now it was time to find a doctor, I thought.

I fainted in the doctor's room, it's funny how I waited until then. I remember walking in to a large room and a very smiley man and feeling exhausted, or was I dizzy? The next thing I remember is waking up on a trolley bed in the same room, attached to a drip. The smiley doctor was still smiling, this time very close to my face. Then he held up a large photo of a group of student doctors for me to see. It was a little too close to make anything out, so he moved it back a little to give me better sight.

"This me in Oxford!" he grinned. "Here I am with medical students, I train there!"

I wasn't sure I could speak yet and raising my eyebrows felt like too much effort, so I didn't do either. He continued.

"I like England very much. You are English yes?"

I managed a nod.

"Look," he pointed to one of the men in the photo he was clutching. "Me!" Then he put it next to his cheek, so I could be sure. His face suddenly morphed into a serious expression, "I am good doctor."

I was glad he was a good doctor, but unsure if his insistence that he was absolutely guaranteed it. My brain was full of wool, and I suddenly noticed how hot I was. My eyes felt like hot, sticky buns cooking in the oven. I moaned.

"Oxford," he mused, looking proudly at his photo. Then he remembered I was there, "Oh and by the way," he said, "I think you have typhoid. I did test. Stay here a few hours. Results in a few days."

Having got a taxi home, slept, thrown up and spent the remaining time on the toilet, I returned when the test results were in. The good doctor who had trained in Oxford proudly showed me my blood test results, which made no sense to me, and nodded in a knowing kind of way.

"See!" He said. "Look at that! I was right."

I looked at the charts, but they wouldn't even have made sense to me without the raging temperature and permanent need to go the bathroom.

"Typhoid?" I thought I should check.

"Yes!" He said gleefully. "Not just that, two other types of salmonella too!" He seemed more pleased than I was at the news.

"But I had a vaccination in England." I protested.

"Doesn't work," he banged his hand on the table.

"Oh." I sighed, "What now?" I felt so awful, I wanted to stay on the bed in his office and have another drip, even if I had to look at his photos again.

"Take these tablets. Two kinds." He handed me the prescription. "You get better!"

"What should I eat?" I couldn't eat without throwing up at the moment but I was relieved it would change with the tablets.

"Eggs!" He smiled big.

"With salmonella? Eggs? Are you sure?"

"Lots of eggs, rice and milk. Next person coming now." He told me as he stood and pointed to the door.

I got steadily worse.

It got increasingly harder to walk until I had to crawl to the toilet on my hands and knees. When that was too much, I pulled myself along the floor, but it took so much energy I would have to stop and rest several times along the way. Sometimes I would fall asleep in the hall before I got to the bathroom. The weight dropped off so violently that friends who came to visit looked more alarmed than a sick person wants their visitors to look. My muscles seemed to be seizing up. My friend, Kat, decided enough was enough and took me back to the doctor.

"I don't think she should be getting worse," she told him.

After he'd shown us his photos again, he told us not to worry because he had another patient with typhoid and reiterated that eggs and milk were the way to go. When Kat questioned the wisdom of that, given my salmonella status, he appeared quite affronted and launched into a five-minute soliloquy on how good the milk in Bolivia is and where it comes from (Potosi cows was his answer, presumably with their heads very much attached to their bodies).

The following day it was decided that another friend, Teresa, take me to a new doctor, who seemed more than a little horrified at the thought of me attempting to eat fried eggs and milk. Not quite so horrified, however, as he was when he saw the tablets I was taking. One was counteracting the other, he explained as I drooped precariously on the edge of a chair. A miserable chicken carcass, little more than half the weight I'd been when I'd left England almost a year earlier.

"The tablets are killing you." Teresa translated. "Well, that and the typhoid."

"Should I be in hospital?" I asked. He shook his head gravely.

"Better not to."

I didn't want to die. I was determined to get better with the help of the new doctor's super-tablets. A week later after many chats with Svenya, soup with Teresa, movies with James and dancing with saucepans from Kat, which I think was meant to come under entertainment, I could stand on my own again and I didn't feel quite as hot for quite so much of the time. I still spent the majority of my day sleeping and the rest of it in the bathroom admiring the bare electric wires in the shower as I sat on the seat now most familiar to me in the house.

I desperately needed a change of scenery and got a taxi down to the Institute, where I was teaching, to sit at their Halloween party for a while. I lurched my way from the taxi door across the sidewalk to the Institute building on the main thoroughfare of La Paz. The harder I tried to get to the door, the further away it seemed to be. My legs seized and I had to swing from my hips to get any movement, as if I had two heavy wooden legs attached to my hips. Passers-by stopped to watch as I struggled to move until my hips refused to work too and I was left clinging to the side of a shop wondering what happens next. It was the strangest feeling to be willing my legs to work but have no response. No matter how hard I willed, or how nicely I spoke to them, my legs stood there trembling, then collapsed.

I don't know how long it was before James rescued me and carried me up to the Halloween party, but I do know I sat in a chair for whole hour or so before dramatically falling to the floor, unconscious. Coming around was terrifying. I blinked my eyes in disbelief as a sea of witches, ghouls and other purveyors of the dark side peered down at me. Typhoid can do some bad things to a person.

I left the party much as I had entered it, this time semi-conscious and spread-eagled over James's shoulder. He put me to bed and heated some of the vat of vegetable soup Teresa had cooked me, then, as I could no longer move my body, attempted to spoon feed me without dribbling it down my neck.

The witches must have done something because after that I started to improve. A month after limping into Dr Death's surgery, I felt strangely clean. Everything I'd ever eaten or drunk must have been cleared from my body ten times over. I felt clear, clean and as delicate as a new-born baby. I was alive! Alive in a way I'd never been before.

To celebrate, I decided to cycle down the Road of Death.

Retrospective top tips on how not to die of typhoid:

- ↘ *If you're sick to the point that you throw up on yourself, it's time to see a doctor*
- ↘ *If your doctor is more interested in showing you photos than telling you about your condition, get a new doctor*
- ↘ *Probably best to avoid eating eggs with a case of salmonella*
- ↘ *Have some friends handy to feed you and give you fireman's lifts*

Lesson Learned

Sometimes what seems terrible can turn out to give you a new lease of life.

SKIDDING OFF THE ROAD OF DEATH
El Camino De La Muerte, Bolivia 2000

Reasons for near-death:
A case of over-enthusiasm; A large red truck;
Death Road.

I lived with two Kiwis in La Paz. Alistair owned a mountain biking company that guided unassuming tourists down 'Death Road,' the other, who was a guide for the company, was very nice, but talked more than anyone else I have ever met. Eventually, she left La Paz to go and talk elsewhere and was replaced by Matt, Alistair's brother and self-confessed, 'ladies' man'.

I liked them both, though I didn't see them that much. I was out most of the time before typhoid, and in my bedroom or the toilet during it. Except when I was sleeping on the hallway floor. Matt was correct in his assertion of being a ladies' man, and most nights, about 12 or 1am, he would creep in, woman in tow, being the loud kind of quiet that only drunk people can manage. I marvelled at how he managed to attract so many women who didn't speak English when he didn't speak Spanish either. After a while I realised just how far you can get using only the word, "Vamos".

I'd vowed never to bike the 64km down Death Road to the colonial town of Coroico, even though Alistair had assured me several times, "You just hev to do it, ay?" The thing about New

Zealanders is that they are very good at making things sound a) fun and b) easy, which makes them perfect for guiding tours down the most dangerous road in the world. The only downside is that their intonation makes most sentences sound like a question. You don't really want your guide on Death Road telling you your brakes are safe in a way that suggests they aren't sure and that perhaps you might know better than they do. ("Your brekes are fine ay?")

I had taken the bus along the terrifyingly high, single-track dirt road when Charlotte and I were returning from the Amazon trip with the angry Dutch man. Crosses people have placed for their loved ones, reminders of the fact that hundreds of people per year die on the road, lie at almost every bend (and a few of the straight parts). The road is carved roughly into the towering cliffs and there are no guard rails separating your vehicle from the 1000 meter drop below. Local drivers are notoriously drunk whilst navigating the cliff edges which certainly leads to an exciting journey. When they're not drunk, they seem anxious to get there at the fastest speed possible. I remember giving Charlotte a blow by blow account of what percentage of tyre below us was hanging over the cliff - until, that is, she announced quite firmly that she didn't feel the need to know. Charlotte was busy watching the driver crossing himself every time we passed a wooden cross, which was quite frequently. This meant he spent half the journey driving with one hand, which wasn't reassuring. It was challenging to focus on something other than the fact that there was a very real possibility of the bus going a millimetre too far over the edge and us all plunging down into the abyss to join the graveyard of buses and cars rotting at the bottom. I wondered what it felt like to fall, there would be a lot of time to feel it if you did. I wondered if anyone had ever survived. I was just wondering what was the furthest someone had ever backed up on the road where it was too narrow to pass another car when the lady in the seat immediately in front of us started gesticulating wildly and mumbling. It took a moment to realise she was crossing herself vigorously and muttering a slew of Hail Marys. We grabbed each other and peered out of the window to find all we could see was green going downwards - a long way. The bus inched past a truck as we sat in silence and I closed my eyes, listening to the chants and the rustle of the lady in front's hurried hand movements. All in all, it was not a relaxing experience and left me with no desire to go back down the treacherous path on a mountain bike. Until I'd recovered from typhoid. My escape from the spindly fingers of death made me want to feel life a bit more. And what better to make you appreciate life than a freewheeling jaunt down the Road of Death?

Kat and I were excited. We were preparing to set off for our trip with a cup of tea in my lounge when we heard my housemate Matt talking to Duncan, one of the other guides, in the hallway. He was explaining the codes they used over the radio to connect with each other. Usually the guides rode at the front and back of the group to make sure everyone was okay, they therefore needed a system of communication. In 2000, it was done through bleeps on their radios.

"Priss it once for, 'how's it going?'" Matt explained, "Two bleeps means there's been an accident, and three means, 'Oh Shut! Panic!' but we never hev to use that one."

Kat and I made a face at each other. "I hope not!" She said grinning.

The starting point is about 4,700 meters above sea level. During the ride, you descend more than 3,600 meters through waterfalls and a forest of cloud until you arrive in the Amazonian jungle. From the bus, I'd seen only the drop below and the woman in front's bobbing head. Here on the bike, open to the elements, it was magical. Looking up the vertical cliff above the road, the rich, green foliage seemed to glow and fill me with life. Looking below and across the pass, the greenery was so dense and verdant it seemed to flow down the cliffs and along the gorge. It was like one massive, powerful, garden of Eden.

We were tearing down the Road of Death! It was incredible. We'd started cautiously, acutely aware of the edge of the road and the vertical precipice below, we took it slow through the thick blanket of cloud, but it wasn't long before we were hurtling down the rocky path squealing and whooping. It's rare that something is so exhilarating that your ego has no choice but to move aside and the only thing you can possibly do is howl with how free and expanded you feel in that moment.

It happened so fast that it seemed to move in slow motion. We probably shouldn't have been freewheeling quite that fast or close to each other and we probably should have slowed down more as we approached the bend. My vision went from expanded open verdure to the front of a large red truck in a split second. It was like the moment in a movie when the predator jumps out at you full screen close up - or in this case, the moment in real life when the front of a bloody great truck appears right in your face. Just one part, because it's too close to see it all. I clawed at my brakes and miraculously skidded sideways around the outside wing of the truck. I tried looking back at Kat who was in the center, but only heard the sickening screech of the brakes and the crash. Then my distorted sense of reality came to land on a protracted dragging sound. It was my body, still attached to my bike, skidding towards the edge of the abyss. There was nothing I could do but watch as the edge of the cliff came gliding towards me. I grappled uselessly at the ground in an effort to stop myself, but the momentum of the bike was too much, all I could do was close my eyes and wait.

There was nothing under one of my legs. I lifted my head and my stomach dropped. My leg, along with the edge of one of my wheels was dangling over 1000 meters of nothing. Carefully, I wriggled my torso until I could feel solid earth under both legs, disentangled from the bike and shaking like a chihuahua, crawled over to the front of the truck. There was no way Kat could have survived a head on crash. My heart was pounding wildly but I was terrified enough that it felt as though it had stopped at the same time. I peered around the front wing. A bicycle lay on the red earth, wheels gently clicking. Kat was nowhere to be seen. Then I caught a movement under the middle of the truck and heard a soft groan as she emerged from beneath the monster that tried to swallow her. My mouth opened and stayed there. How the hell was she moving, let alone alive? She'd somehow flipped over the top of her bike and skidded neatly between the front wheels of the broad-shouldered truck. There were shouts and animated voices as the truck driver, and Duncan, who was at the back of the group pulled her out and sat her on the road to assess her injuries. I was still too shaky to walk, so I crawled over and sat next to her, vibrating. She was battered and bruised but the only source of blood seemed to be her knee. I saw Duncan signal two bleeps on his radio to Matt at the front - there's been an accident - then he ran to the group bus that had appeared, it was following behind to bring the bikes back afterwards. He grabbed the first aid kit and ran back over, kneeling down to bathe and dress the deep gash on her knee. I've never been great with injuries, not because I'm afraid of them, but because I seem to have a fascination with what they look like, which doesn't always feel good to the person nursing the wound. I peered down at Kat's knee while Duncan was getting the kit.

"I can see bone!" I said helpfully. Except Kat didn't find it helpful. She was just telling me how unhelpful it was when three long bleeps came over Duncan's radio. We looked at each other. Three was the disaster one wasn't it? Duncan looked down at the radio a second, then shrugged.

"Nah," he said. "It's nothing."

"Three means something bad happened right?" Kat offered.

"Yeah, but it'll be a mistake." He bathed and dressed her knee, then bandaged it with the kind of expertise you'd expect someone learning how to dress a zombie for the first time to have. He was about to help her stand up when three, long, clear beeps came over the radio again followed by a crackly,

"Git down here now."

Duncan ran, jumped on his bike and shouted to the bus driver to help us follow on behind.

The bigger disaster took over our adrenalin and our psyche immediately. We helped each other up shakily and retrieved our bikes.

"Are you going to ride or get in the bus?" the driver asked hastily as the truck driver said his relieved goodbyes and left.

"We'll bike," Kat decided much to my surprise. And because the situation was a three-bleep disaster and we were only a two, we got straight back on our bikes and rode down towards the rest of the group, a few hairpin bends away. I was shaking so hard, I couldn't hold the handlebars steady and I noticed Kat wasn't able to use her leg, but we kept going until we reached the crowd, lined up along the edge of the cliff, their faces stained with terror.

Nick, a reporter on the Bolivian Times had approached the corner too fast, tried to brake, and much to the horror of those behind him, skidded off the edge of Death Road.

I would not have wanted to be the first person brave enough to lie down, peer over the crumbling verge and down into the abyss of certain death. Whoever it was found Nick and his bike suspended on a lone tree jutting out at a right angle from the side of the gorge.

All we could do was sit and shake while we watched the rescue operation. Nick, his girlfriend, Kat and I rode the rest of the way in the bus as none of us were in any kind of shape to control a bike. When we arrived at the bottom, Nick was whisked off to hospital to find he'd escaped with smashed teeth, several impressive gashes but no broken bones. Luckily for him, the people at the hospital were better with bandages than Duncan. Kat didn't go to hospital. We had learned from others that Bolivian hospitals are a last resort, not a first (or a second or third). Even the doctor in La Paz had advised against it.

Delirious with the fact that we were still alive and at the same time, still in shock, Kat and I found a room in a hostel in Coroico with a pool looking out over the lush Amazonian mountains. It came with a German man who had to pass through our room to get to his and felt it was unnecessary to knock at any time of day or night.

We wandered the main town square, buzzing with street sellers and the comings and goings of all kinds of people. We met a charming Austrian man who couldn't stop talking and insisted on calling the town 'Creekycoco', convinced he'd got it down right and uninterested in suggestions otherwise. Then we found a promising restaurant and consumed untold amounts of banana pancakes and mashed potatoes until the kitchen staff came out to see who was eating so much. Our eyes were bigger than our bellies, or the trauma of the day had caught up and wanted us to eat in an effort to avoid thinking about it. Either way, we lumbered out, weighed down by carbohydrates, and fell into our beds groaning as our stomachs gurgled.

The following morning, we were woken by the German guy who didn't believe in knocking. He felt it was important to let us know that there was, 'much bad air' in our room and saw fit to lean over my bed and open the window. I guess anyone willing to consume large amounts of mashed potatoes and banana pancakes should expect to be party to bad air of some sort as a result.

The two of us took a local minibus back along El Camino De La Muerte the following day under the premise that a minibus was less likely to go over than a larger coach type bus. At the time, there was no other road back to La Paz. Unfortunately, we were late arriving which made us unpopular with the other passengers. The journey passed away relatively uneventfully until we stopped to stretch our legs. We extracted ourselves from the bus the only way you can from South American minibuses - a kind of 'being birthed' exit in which you attempt to gather yourself, your elongated arms and legs and your backpack together and push them through a hole not big enough for one of them much less all of them. Although it's a struggle, the sense of achievement when you finally make it out is rewarding.

I stood on the edge of the world, breathing in the crisp, clear air, looking out across a sea of lush green. I'd survived! I'd survived typhoid and I'd survived nearly skidding off Death Road!

"Life is good!" I thought, as the sound of drumming water entered my awareness. I turned around to find a stray dog using my pack as a toilet - much to everyone's amusement. Though unfortunate, this made us much more popular, and for the remainder of the journey the locals amused themselves by smiling at me, pointing at my bag and laughing a lot. It wasn't quite how I'd envisaged my triumphant return to La Paz having cycled El Camino De La Muerte, but I guessed it would have to do.

Retrospective top tips on how not to die on Death Road:

- ➘ *Don't go - this is the only guarantee*
- ➘ *Try not to get carried away with the exhilaration and forget that it is, in fact, called Death Road for a reason*
- ➘ *Ride slow*

Lesson Learned

Slow down and enjoy the scenery.

A SERIES OF UNFORTUNATE EVENTS
South Africa/Lesotho 1990

Reasons for near-death:
Getting the wrong bus; A series of most
unfortunate events.

"There's only one bus to Lesotho. Over there. Night bus. Leaves in two hours."

The information guy at the small station in Durban pointed to a bench. A couple of people stood next to it, presumably waiting for the Lesotho bus.

"How long does it take?"

He shrugged and hesitated before settling on, "Many hours."

I said goodbye to my traveling companions, made my way over to the waiting area, took my small pack off and sat on the bench to wait.

My aim was to go trekking on the stout Basotho ponies through the mountain kingdom of Lesotho. I'd met a couple of girls during my travels up the South-Western coast of South Africa who'd described the beauty of the small landlocked country. A nation made entirely of mountains was enticing, plus I was looking forward to seeing if I could stay on a pony longer than I'd ever managed to stay on a horse.

By the time the bus pulled up, I was tired. I noticed that something felt off as I climbed the steel steps and made my way along the aisle to one of only two empty seats, but I ignored the feeling because I just wanted to sit down and get to Lesotho. I could tell it wasn't going to be a comfortable journey, there was very little padding left in my seat and even though I tried stuffing the sad foam, spilling out of a large split, back inside the cover, it splurged out again as if it had simply grown too big to be confined. I settled in and the bus rattled off, juddering and jolting along the asphalt. What would it be like when we got to the dirt roads in the country I wondered as I made eye contact with a woman sitting a couple of rows in front. I smiled. She gave me a stony stare in return then pointedly turned her head forwards. That was when I became aware that people were looking at me in the kind of way that doesn't feel comfortable. I glanced behind to a sea of faces glaring at me and quickly turned back to stare out the window. What had I done? Then a man from the seat across the aisle shuffled over next to me and, staring ahead, muttered, "Not safe. White girl no travel on bus for black tribes."

Oh my God, what had I done! So naive, it hadn't crossed my mind that in the insane political and social climate, it wouldn't be okay for me to travel on this bus. Nelson Mandela had just been released and my unworldly eighteen-year old self had presumed that it meant everything was instantly going to be okay. The guy next to me was still looking forwards as if he wasn't talking to me.

"Should I get off?" I muttered.

"No chance, next stop Lesotho. Be careful." He said before shifting back to his original seat.

My heart sat in my throat for the next few hours as I shrunk down and tried to make myself as inconspicuous as possible. Suddenly a cry went up from the people behind and a surge of shuffling started. I stole a glance and saw people hurriedly picking up their bags as a stream of urine meandered along the floor my side. I grabbed my bag just as it reached my feet. Five minutes later, we stopped beside a block of toilets at the side of the highway, presumably the driver wanted to prevent the same thing happening again.

I got off last, trying not to be noticed or get in anyone's way and followed the last person over the grass verge to the toilets. The man who'd spoken to me as if we were having a secret mafia meeting on the bus, pointed to a sign that said, "Whites." I stopped and stared at it. This was all so alien to me.

Embarrassed to be different, I turned left towards the 'white' toilet, while everyone else turned right. I half-ran, half-walked down the mud path to find the toilet door shut and locked with a padlock. I rattled at it just in case, but it was definitely not coming undone. My bladder was bursting. I went to squat down on the grass, but a rustling behind me sent a rod of fear through my chest and I ran back up to the road. The only option, as I saw it, was to go to the 'black' toilets. I followed the sign around to the right and entered through a large brick doorway.

The scene was incredible, a huge square room, with what seemed like hundreds of people sitting on benches that lined the walls, chatting. A second layer of benches further in was also full. Animated voices rung out and bounced off the walls, joining somewhere in the middle as one continuous sound. It reminded me of a Roman scene for some reason. I gaped in awe, forgetting that I was the odd one out and it took a while for me to hear the sound slowly dying down as people began to notice my presence. I looked around to see a doorway in the wall to my left marked, *women,* and headed over determinedly.

Inside, I recognized a few women from the bus as we queued.

"The other toilets were closed." I offered by way of explanation as I tried not to look at the four people going to the toilet in the stalls that had no doors. No one answered, though I did see a few raised eyebrows. Later, when I traveled to China and had to sit on a hole in the ground with people either side of me doing the same and no stalls to be seen, much less doors, I remembered these toilets and how hard I had found it to pee with people standing in line pointedly watching me. Little did I know, it was much easier than peeing while the person next to you, also peeing, is so close that your arms touch. It's hard to let go.

Everyone should experience the feeling of being 'the only one' of something they cannot change. There's no way you can imagine the feeling and sometimes the fear that can come with it. This experience changed my understanding of many things I had previously been oblivious to.

Back on the bus, I started to feel thirsty. I'd cleverly not brought water or food with me for the overnight journey, thinking I could get some on the way. It was dusky out now and as we bumped our way along the highway, I felt a desperation for the sleep that wouldn't come. Suddenly, a bang, loud as a gunshot rang out, the bus lurched sideways, skidded and bumped as the driver tried to control it. Shouts and bellows filled the bus until we slowed and jerked, finally coming to a stop as traffic whizzed around us. Everyone filed off the bus and we stood on the hard shoulder of the motorway while a group of men argued about the tyre that had burst. I stood back from the traffic and watched until a few of the men came sweeping towards me shouting angrily in a language I couldn't understand. My organs contracted until I was sure they'd swallowed themselves, but I didn't move or say anything, mostly because I couldn't. A couple of others came to pull them away and as soon as I could breathe again, I backed off along the hard shoulder until I was in full view of the passing cars. A BMW screeched to a halt right where I was standing. The window opened and a face appeared.

"Not safe for you here." The man said in an African accent. "Where are you going?"

I told him. He hesitated a second and turned to the women in the passenger seat before saying, "Get in, we will take you."

I looked at him. Which was safer? To stay on the bus, or get into a car with a couple I didn't know?

"I'll get my bag." I said and ran back to the bus where I retrieved my pack, heart pounding. By the time I returned, I couldn't see the car for the crowd of passengers gathered around it. Some grappled with the back door handles until the car revved and took off down the motorway with an almighty screech.

I watched the taillights disappear and felt tears stinging at my eyes. Okay, I said to myself, breathing deeply, maybe it's for the best, maybe the bus is safer. And because I didn't want to stand on the grass and risk being shouted at again, I got back on the bus and tried to pretend I wasn't there.

Things were relatively quiet when we finally got going again. I was too scared to sleep and instead kept my eye on the two men who'd been so angry with me. My head was aching when we arrived at the border with Lesotho, but I didn't care, I'd made it! Thank God.

A policeman climbed up the steps of the bus, looking over the heads of the passengers disapprovingly, he spoke to the driver in an African language before his eyes landed on me. He raised his eyebrows slowly and gestured towards me. I stood and walked to the front.

"Passport." He barked.

I went back to get it from my bag, but before I got there, he bellowed down the bus,

"Bring bag and passport. Come with me."

I followed him off the bus with a sigh of relief. I wouldn't have to get back on! I could cross the border here and find my way to a hostel. I sat down in the small office while the policeman looked at my documents. Out the window, I could see the bus moving into a parking space rather than going through the border gate and wondered what was happening. Half an hour later, the policeman approached me.

"Follow me." He commanded. We walked through the office and out a door, hanging on for life by one hinge, into a car park at the back. I started to feel nervous, though I wasn't sure why. My headache was still there, maybe it was the adrenalin.

"Can I cross the border now?" I asked.

He shook his head and beckoned me to keep following, weaving around the parked cars, then stopped. That was the moment I knew something was terribly wrong. I felt as though someone's hand closed around my throat, pulling me back, choking me. I looked at him and tried to swallow, he had my passport in his hand. Something made me put my pack on my back.

"Can I have my passport please?" I tried to make my voice level, but it was strangled.

He smiled, a lascivious smile. "No," and looked me right in the eyes. It made me want to throw up.

He grabbed me with one hand and opened the car door with the other.

"You're coming home with me." He said, laughing loudly, "You are mine." He pushed me easily into the opening, but my pack hit the doorway and he had to readjust to get me in.

Something deep inside me rose up. I felt it roar with outrage. Indignation burned through my body giving me strength beyond anything I'd felt before. I screamed in his face, kicked him hard and thrashed out, pushing him backwards until I was out. My passport fell as he tripped and I grabbed it, kicked again, roared with anger and ran.

I ran for my life, dodging through the cars without looking back. I couldn't make any sense of what was ahead of me as I scanned around to find a safe place. Policeman were dotted around but now came under, 'not safe'. I weaved and swerved, there were shouts behind me. Then I saw the bus, and without another thought headed for it. My chest was burning but I kept running, finally hitting the door with a thud. I banged hard on it, desperate to get back to the seat that had seemed so unsafe earlier. The driver looked at me, confused. I banged again.

"Please!" I mouthed through the doors as he frowned at me and finally opened them. I climbed up the steps, muttered a thank you and staggered to my ripped seat, now a place of sanctuary. My breath rasped painfully as I tried to control it and ignore the stares. The doors closed, engine roared and the bus moved off. I looked out the window searching for the policeman, wondering if he'd stop us. There he was, watching us leave, a big smile on his face as he laughed.

I was shaking so hard it took a good hour to calm down, which meant I didn't even question where we were going until then. It was pitch black outside now and must have been *many hours* (as the guy in the information office in Durban said) since we'd left. I hadn't eaten or drunk anything. I sidled over to the edge of the seat and looked at the guy who'd spoken to me earlier.

"Where are we going?" I whispered. It was the first time I'd noticed that no-one had gone through the border.

He whispered back through the dim lights on the bus. "Not allowed in. Wrong tribe. Must go another border. Many hours." And that was the end of our conversation.

We bumped and jogged our way over dirt roads for another few hours. My headache had progressed and was splitting my head in two. I needed water, but there wasn't any so I'd have to wait. I had no idea where we were, I just needed to hold on and get to the next border crossing. My thoughts ran wildly through my throbbing head and my nervous system screamed along with the squeaks and screeches of the bus. Then we stopped. The engine died down, lights went dark and everyone gradually filed off the bus in silence. I peered into the inky blackness through the window. Where were we? There was nothing here. They were probably going to the bathroom again, but I had no desire to go and stayed on the bus, waiting. No one came back. About half an hour later, head pounding, I decided to see where they'd gone and whether there was any liquid there. I was getting desperate.

We were in a field, as far as I could make out. I rounded the bus, there was nothing here. As I came back to the front of the bus, I noticed a light burning, way in the distance. I guess that's where they are, I shrugged, and my desperation for something to drink made me head for the light.

As I approached the glow, I heard music, drumming that seemed to beat with my heart, faster and faster. This time it was like something from a movie. I appeared in the doorway to find a large open area on my left where men were drumming, chanting and dancing in tribal dress. On my right, were benches where men and women were drinking and chatting.

The drumming stopped.

The chanting died.

The chatting faded away.

Everyone turned to stare at me in silence. I gazed out in horror at the sea of wide, unfriendly eyes and tried to make my brain work out the best thing to do. Running would be stupid, I settled on showing I wasn't a threat instead.

The bar was at the back of the structure. I took a deep breath, steadied myself and walked through the crowd to the bar. The crowd parted like the red sea. Still no-one made a sound. The journey seemed to take an age, I was floating, then I heard my voice as though it were coming through a loud speaker.

"I'd like a coke please."

A shadow on my right made me look up. A tall African man in tribal dress, at least six foot three loomed over me. He looked me in the eyes, put a finger to his throat and gestured slicing it from one side to the other.

I ran.

I legged it out and back across the field. I could hear people running after me and men shouting to each other. I ran. That same strength I'd felt only hours earlier roared up from deep within and I sprinted faster than I'd ever imagined I could. The voices were still behind me, closer, shouting and laughing now. I could see the bus - but running onto the bus would only trap me as I couldn't close the door, so I turned towards a small hut I could just make out through the first light of a murky dawn. 20 meters now, 10, 5, I prayed it had a lock inside as the sounds of the men behind me got closer.

I grabbed at the door, flung my heaving body inside, shut it and - thank God - locked it just as one of the men reached me and started banging and shaking the door. It seemed to be holding up as they hammered on it, so I turned to see where I was. The stench hit me like a brick wall. Tiny streams of dawn poked through the ceiling onto a large heap of diarrhoea around a hole in the ground. I threw up again and again, adding to the mess of bodily fluids, listening to the sound of the men talking and laughing outside the locked door.

When my stomach stopped heaving, I waited. I would probably miss the bus, but I'd have to work that out later, there was no way I was leaving the safety of a locked door. I leaned my hot head on the wood and closed my eyes, talking to myself gently as I did. It was going to be okay. They would get bored soon and leave. I was going to get out of this.

Some time later, the voices grew fainter until I could no longer hear them. I waited another 10 minutes or so, then slowly slid the lock aside and peered out into the dawn. No-one. And there was the bus! I checked all directions, then charged across the muddy field to the bus, once again, my sanctuary. This time I crouched down under my seat, so my head couldn't be seen through the window. About an hour later, voices chopped at the air outside and I peered up to see the bus passengers making their way back. I wanted to be invisible, but the best I could do was not look at anyone as they piled back onto the steel carriage. I held my breath until they were all in and thanked life that nobody had approached me.

This was it, surely this was it and we were now going to the border, one we could get across, one without policeman trying to kidnap me, one where I could find a drink and a bed. My head thrashed and my eyes watered, but I couldn't feel anything above the adrenalin.

Hours later, we rattled into the border at Maseru. Once again, I was taken off the bus by police, this time handed over to the young man in uniform at the hut right on the border gateway. It was the kind of open gate you find in a car park, a long barrier that lifts up and down. He smiled at me, all teeth.

"Passport."

I gave it to him. He checked it out, asked me a couple of questions, nodding sagely as I answered. Then he told me to wait at the side of the road and disappeared into his hut. A couple of minutes later, he emerged without my passport and went to attend the people waiting in their cars to cross the border. I watched a while before walking over to him.

"Can I have my passport please?"

He shook his head seriously and went to talk to the folks in the next car. The bus was third in line. He talked to the driver and a few of the passengers, then let them through. I watched as they disappeared up the long hill. After the fourth vehicle went through, I approached him again.

"Let me through." I said, past pleases and thank yous now.

"First," he wrote something on the paper on his clipboard, "you must tell me you love me."

I was done. Something had snapped in me a while ago and I no longer cared.

"NO." I said, raising my voice, "give me my passport. Now."

"No." He went to see the next in line before coming back. "Ready?" he asked. I shook my head. "Fuck you." I said. He shrugged.

When he sauntered over the third time, he informed me that he was going to marry me.

I waited another 10 minutes, my breath rising in tandem with my exasperation. I knew my passport was in his hut next to the border gate. I watched, feeling a power swell inside me. He was talking to the next car full of people when I bolted for the hut and time went into slow motion. I reached the doorway; my passport was sitting on the counter. I heard him shouting behind me as I snatched at it with one hand, still running, I summoned everything I had and leaped over the barrier, stumbling as I landed. I couldn't stop now, I had to run, I had to get up the hill. He was yelling behind me, but I didn't look back, I galloped up the hill, spluttering and choking for breath the further up I got. Finally, I stopped to check behind me. There was no-one there. He'd let me go. I collapsed at the side of the road gasping to get my breath back until it calmed.

I wish I could say that was it. I went pony trekking in the land of mountains and had the time of my life, but that was not to be. Instead, I staggered up the hill until I found a white building at the side of the road with the word, 'hostel' outside. I heaved a sigh of relief and checked myself in, not realising I was the only one there. Sleep was what I needed. The owner showed me to the dorm of bunk beds and said I could choose, then disappeared. It was simple and not that clean, but it looked like heaven to me. I pulled back the sheets and shrieked. It was crawling with cockroaches. Not one or two, there were at least 20 dancing around under that sheet. I tried another bed, and another, each had its own insect party going on. I called for the owner, but he was nowhere to be seen. Finally, I turned, picked up my pack and left.

I was wrung out like a wet rag. Water, food and sleep were so needed, but I wanted safety first. I no longer knew what was okay and what wasn't, the streets I walked had a dreamlike quality and seemed to shake at the edges. I couldn't think straight.

I'd wandered for a while, hoping to find another hostel when a car horn made me jump. I turned to see an American man, in his 30s, beckoning me over. He was a doctor and had been living in the area for some time. I told him a little about the bus and my need for a hostel and in return, he told me it was a very dangerous time and that I should get the hell out.

"Go back to the border and hitch out with a family," he advised.

"I can't! I don't want to see the border guy again." I protested, but he assured me the *out* border was different from the *in* one, then gave me a lift to it.

"Remember," he called through the car window, "only a family with children."

My dreams of mountains and ponies faded easily as I stood at the side of the crossing waiting for a family, feeling a bit like a vulture. It was at least an hour before I spotted one and darted over to ask if they would take me to wherever they were going as long as it was a town. They retreated to discuss it for a while, then called me over. They'd take me as far as they could.

I got in, relieved. I wasn't in the mood to talk much, though I tried a little before falling asleep mid-sentence. Next I knew, the mum was shaking me awake.

"You have to get out here." She said, her Afrikaans accent strong.

I jolted awake, still on alert and stumbled out the car as she handed me my pack from the trunk.

"You'll have to hitch from here." She called as she got back into the front seat and the car sped off.

Strange. I wasn't quite awake, but as I blinked my heavy eye-lids and took in my surroundings, the realisation hit me like a brick wall. I was in the middle of nowhere. Literally. I turned to look behind at fields, as far as the eye could see. Left and right was a road, nothing either side, no buildings, no people, nothing. I dropped my pack in disbelief. Why would they do this? Where the hell was I?

The tears that needed to come out so badly stung at the edges of my eyes, but I couldn't give in yet, I had to keep going. Survival instinct is strong, and I took some deep breaths, told myself calmly I was going to make it out alive and worked out what to do next. It wasn't hard. The only thing to do was hitch. With a family I guessed, though that hadn't worked out so well. I discussed it with myself aloud, which felt reassuring, and decided I would simply hitch and if I felt safe when they opened the door, I would get in, otherwise I would refuse. I stuck out my thumb.

I refused four cars that stopped. A lone man, two minibuses and two men in a flash car. They were all understandably annoyed that they had stopped and now I was telling them I didn't want to get in. I was calm and firm, determined to be clear in myself what was safe. The fifth car was another minibus. My heart sank as the door slid open to a sea of grinning men. I looked around at the overstuffed seats when I heard a voice boom out from the back of the bus.

"Well hello! Come in, we have room here. You look thirsty.

Want a drink of water?" There, trying to shove people up to make room for me was a woman, larger than life, a voice like treacle, her skirts billowing down to the floor and a headscarf wrapped ornately around her hair. She was an angel, well, she seemed that way to me as she held out a bottle of water and smiled, her teeth bright against the brown of her face. I climbed in and squeezed my way over to her, unable to stop the tears of relief.

"It's okay." She put her arm around me. "You safe." And I fell asleep on her ample bosom.

I didn't care that we broke down twice because she was there, talking and laughing and looking out for me.

They dropped me off in the city of Bloemfontein where I got a train ticket for the next day and collapsed in a hotel room to sleep for 14 hours straight.

Retrospective top tips on how not to die on a bus trip from Durban to Lesotho:

- ↘ *Don't trust the guy at the information desk in Durban bus station*
- ↘ *Take plenty of food and water*
- ↘ *Listen to your gut*
- ↘ *Look out for your guardian angel*

Lesson Learned

When something feels 'off', listen to that feeling.

WHITE WATER WHIRLPOOL WONDER
Bhote Kosi River, Nepal, 2000

Reasons for near-death:
Attempting to tackle a set of rapids without a raft;
A vicious whirlpool.

Hiking up to Langtang in the Himalaya had been challenging. It wasn't the hiking that was challenging so much as the severe case of giardia I had taken with me. Finding convenient places to have diarrhoea on mountains is not in my top ten list of things I enjoy. Having diarrhoea in blizzard conditions half-way up when the toilet is an outside shack is even less enjoyable. I dug my way through waist-height snow to the toilet at least once an hour, while Penny, my trekking partner, shovelled yak shit on the fire. Nevertheless, we made it there just in time to get stuck in another blizzard for four days before finally staggering back down, now both heavily under the influence of diarrhoea.

High on the achievement of making it back to Kathmandu, once things had died down in the toilet department, I thought I'd have a go at white water rafting.

Kathmandu is magical. The old town feels ancient. The time-worn stone buildings, the stalls selling bloody carcasses, and the medieval temples seem to reach out and pull you back into the past. I was mesmerised by the colors, sights and sounds. Some say

Kathmandu is a sensory overload but it's a more-gentle, less chaotic overload than India. If you're thinking of going to India, Nepal is a good place to start - a practice run in the sensory department. Nepal feels grounded. It's crazy at times, perplexing, beautiful and deeply peaceful. The people have peace shining in their eyes. It made me feel as though anything is possible. 'What better place to try my hand at rafting than on a wild river overlooked by Mount Everest?' I declared, and booked myself in with the young local guys offering a trip at half the price of any other.

I didn't think about why it was so cheap until we set off. We were to begin our travel to the Bhote Kosi river on the roof of a crowded local bus. I was up for it, and climbed up the ladder, finding a place near the middle to settle in. The view was quite something from up there, and I was happily staring down at the colorful, chaotic towns of Nepal when one of the locals grabbed my head and shoved it down onto the rumbling steel roof. I sat up in indignation but saw everyone else was squashed flat against the peeling blue paint and ducked limbo style just in time to miss the electric cables hanging overhead. After that I watched the locals, who at regular intervals only briefly paused their conversations to flatten themselves and avoid death by electrocution. I ducked as soon as they did. Being that close to electric cables and avoiding certain death so frequently gave me an odd feeling of freedom. My life was literally in my hands, one second too slow on the dodging and that was it. I'd had a similar feeling in La Paz every time I tried to cross the road. Health and Safety rules have their obvious benefits, but there are hidden disadvantages. There is a great sense of fulfilment that comes with being responsible for yourself.

At the river, the young guides set up the two rafts. We were to be six to a raft plus the guide. The area was stunning, deep green forests running down to the riverside. I breathed in the clean air, stared up at the mountains and listened to the roar of the rapids before wondering briefly whether not being able to swim was a problem.

"Careful." Said the guide in our pre-rapid pep talk. "These rapids danger. Four and Five. If fall out, get back in quick."

I put my hand up. "Does it matter that I can't swim?"

A look of horror crossed his face before he laughed, "You have life vest." He said to reassure himself. I considered not going for a moment, but there was no other way to get down the river now, so I determined to be careful, like he'd said. I stepped into the second raft and took my seat at the back, paddle in hand.

We were only two rapids down when we hit a rock and I was thrown back head over heels. In their concentrated fervour, the rest of the crew didn't notice me flip off the rear of the raft. In fact, they didn't notice I was gone until they finished the entire set of rapids. That left me to negotiate level 4 and 5 rapids in the water, as a non-swimmer. To be fair, I'm not sure knowing how to swim would have made a difference. The water sucked me in and spat me out mercilessly, flinging me down rapid after rapid. There was no time for swimming, and very little for breathing. The gushing water tossed me into rock after rock, like a rag doll while I struggled to find something to grab until my strength was gone and I had no choice but to let the river hurl me wherever it wanted me to go.

As the rapids eased into calmer waters, I saw the rafts ahead, the terrified faces of those scouring the water for me accentuated in the bright sunlight.

'I made it!' I thought, as a huge whirlpool sucked me down into the depths of the river, spinning and tossing me deeper and deeper, faster and faster until I no longer knew which way was up. I found new strength to struggle and fight against the spinning mass of water, until there was nothing left, and I knew I had lost. I had to breathe, couldn't hold on any longer.

The moment I decided to let go and breathe in the cool, clear water, a divine calm filled my being. Everything stood still. My mind became as crystal clear as the water and I had forever to think, "It's okay. I'm going to die now."

I prepared to take a deep, liquid breath and as I did so, saw the most beautiful sunlight I had ever seen. It was exquisite. I breathed.

My body shot out of the water, something propelling me ver-tically into the air, like a rocket. The sun hit my face full on as I gulped the cool, mountain air into my lungs. The quiet calm evaporated and a thousand thoughts came pommeling back into my head, dulling the crisp clearness of my mind.

Panicked voices and terrified shouts filled my ears and a rope was flying through the air towards me. I caught it easily and held on as I was pulled to the riverbank and dragged onto the rocks by several guides. I lay there, unable to speak. Everyone seemed terrified, yet for a few golden minutes, I felt ecstatic. I could still feel that sunlight under the water and the deep sense of clarity and calm. I let everyone crowd around and heard them re-telling the story to each other as I tried to hang on to the feeling for as long as I could. It was like trying to hold sand in a sieve and I could only watch as it trickled away until I started to shake and felt the cuts and bruises from crashing against the rocks on the way down. The guides were clearly still shocked and tried to reassure me as they dressed my wounds, but I could see them shaking almost as much as I was.

It was one of the hardest things I've done to get back in the raft, but there was only one way out and that was down the river. I climbed back in, took a deep breath and lifted my paddle, ready.

This experience has since become one of the biggest sources of encouragement in my life. Both as a reminder of the peace that can be present in the face of death, and as an understanding that when we're not finished, life will find a way to bring us back. Then there's the getting back into the boat… I don't think the need to do that ever ends, it's just part of life.

Retrospective top tips on how not to die white water rafting:

- *Learn to swim*
- *Don't take the cheapest trip*
- *Avoid whirlpools*

Lesson Learned

Let go, life has got me.

Acknowledgements

Thanks to Uma Devi and Connie Lambrecht for being my first response readers. Kimberly Von Dohren thank you for your constant encouragement and for laughing at my stories. Cameron and Elliot Jayne, thanks for being enthusiastic about my stories. Tristan Lee, thanks for always being there when I come back. And thanks to my brother, Barry and his wife Vic, who sent me off with a credit card for emergencies and a mix tape in 1999.

Oh and to the Metropole Hotel in Padstow, Cornwall, I'm grateful you let me set up home in the chair in the corner for a few weeks. The tea and the wine were lovely.

AUTHOR BIO

Amanda Jayne never wanted to live a normal life, which she has achieved with resounding success so far. Her love for travel began with a six month South Africa trip at age 18 and continued with short jaunts in Eastern Europe during the years she worked in the mental health field. Realizing offices, rules and regulations were not her thing, she left her native England in 1999 to find out more about the world and the amazing array of people living in it. She lived in various countries and finally returned to the UK in 2009 after gaining a masters in Spiritual Psychology in the USA and walking 1,200 km around the 88 temples pilgrimage in Shikoku, Japan.

These days she teaches health and emotional wellness workshops and writes books. Some of the things she loves are trees, art, making up stories for her nephews, heart circles, karaoke, cats and dark chocolate, not necessarily in that order. She lives in a quiet corner of Kent in the UK and tries, but usually fails, to stay there for long periods of time.

Find out more about what she's up to at

www.amandacjayne.com

CPSIA information can be obtained
at www.ICGtesting.com
Printed in the USA
LVHW10s1519150818
587061LV00011B/335/P